Collins

EXPLORE ENGLISH

Student's Resource Book 4

Contents

1 Fun and games
Time to relax (Week 1) — 4
Interesting hobbies (Week 1) — 5
A Hike in the Park (Week 2) — 6–7
Games around the world (Week 3) — 8
Word games (Week 3) — 9

2 Is it true?
In the rainforest (Week 1) — 10–11
Bugs Are Helpful (Week 2) — 12–13
Animals from another time (Week 3) — 14–15

3 Fire!
The Great Fire of London (Week 1) — 16–17
Firefighters (Week 2) — 18
Fire safety! (Week 2) — 19
Puff, the Dragonsaurus (Week 3) — 20–22

4 Animal stories
Peter and the Wolf (Week 1) — 23–25
The Pied Piper of Hamelin (Week 2) — 26–27
Help! The Sky Is Falling (Week 3) — 28–29

5 Our wonderful world
More about our world (Week 1) — 30–31
Built wonders of the world (Week 2) — 32–34
Natural wonders of the world (Week 3) — 35–37

6 The Olympic Games
The Olympics in ancient times (Week 1) — 38–39
From ancient to modern (Week 2) — 40–41
Going for gold! (Week 3) — 42
The odd Olympics (Week 3) — 43

7 Communicating with others
Our eyes and ears (Week 1) — 44–45
Braille – reading by feeling (Week 2) — 46–47
Helen Keller (Week 3) — 48–49

8 Thoughts, feelings and opinions
Fashion forward (Week 1) — 50–51
Jia's diary (Week 2) — 52
Clubs (Week 2) — 53
A Future Celebrity Chef? (Week 3) — 54
Headlines! (Week 3) — 55

9 Let's go on holiday!
Anjali's diary (Week 1) — 56–58
Island fun (Week 2) — 59
An island holiday (Week 2) — 60
Holiday island activities (Week 2) — 61
Where will you go? (Week 3) — 62–63

About this book

This book is full of interesting texts for you to enjoy.

- You can read and discuss modern and traditional **stories**.

The Piper played his flute and the rats ran towards him.

'Hey, Mum! I know what I want to be when I grow up! A fashion designer!'

- You can read **information** about people, places and animals.

Every zebra has its own striped pattern and they sleep standing up.

Usain Bolt – the fastest man in the world!

- There are **poems** to read aloud, perform and enjoy.

- There are **games** to play.

Bugs!
We're everywhere.
We're in the water,
We're in the air.

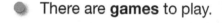

Carol.

Clever, caring Carol.

The same letter word-game

This tells you there is something to **talk** about.

This tells you there is something to **think** about.

Enjoy the book!

Time to relax

We asked some children what they do in their free time.
Read what they said.

Naeem's report

Free time is fun time. It is not time to do homework or chores. I like to be active in my free time. I play tennis and I go swimming. Sometimes I go for a hike with my dad. He is very fit and he makes me walk very fast. Sometimes I am lazy and I spend my free time watching TV. I love watching shows about nature and science.

Nina's report

Free time is quiet time for me to relax. I like to spend my free time on my own. I sit at my desk and play computer games. Sometimes I play against my friend, Desi, but other times I play on my own. I also like to read and draw. If it is cold and rainy I jump into bed and read books or magazines.

How do you like to spend your free time? Do you prefer to be alone or spend time with others?

Interesting hobbies

Read about two interesting hobbies.

A hobby is something that you enjoy doing in your free time. Some people bake, some people paint and some people build models as their hobby. What do you do?

ToyVoyagers – travelling toys

A ToyVoyager is a toy that you send on a journey around the world without you. To do this as a hobby, you register a toy on the ToyVoyager website. They give it a special travel tag and an identity number. After you have registered, you give the toy to someone who is going on a journey. They take photos of your toy in the places they visit and send the photographs and some information to the ToyVoyager site. They later give the toy to someone else to take on a different journey. The toys travel all over the world in this way. You can share your toy's adventures by checking the ToyVoyager website.

Geocaching (say 'jee-oh-cah-shing')

Geocaching involves hunting for hidden containers, called geocaches. People hide the containers in interesting places in the environment and give GPS information for other people to find them. When you find one, you open the container and take the small treasure that is inside. You leave a new treasure for the next person and write your name and other details in the log book. Then you put the geocache back so other people can find it. Geocaching takes place all over the world. This hobby is a fun way for families to get into the outdoors and learn more about places around them.

Where would you hide a geocache in your area? Why do you think that is a good place?

A Hike in the Park

Listen and follow.

Then read the poem again on your own.

What things can you see when you go on a hike?

Last week I went for a hike in Forest Park.
I packed a torch in case it got dark.
I packed my sweater and my lunch,
In case I needed something to munch.

But as I walked, I heard a strange sound –
A shuffle, a scuffle, but when I turned round
There was absolutely nothing there
Just bright green grass and clear fresh air.

I walked on and up. I jumped over rivers.
I kicked down a rock – it gave me the shivers.
For what if the rock knocked somebody flat?
I really, truly wouldn't want that!

Still, every so often, I heard a strange sound –
A shuffle, a scuffle, but when I turned round
There was absolutely nothing there
Just bright green grass and clear fresh air.

I walked behind a small waterfall.
And luckily for me, I'm not very tall.
So I kept myself safe and stayed almost dry
I'm glad the waterfall wasn't that high.

Still, every so often, I heard a strange sound –
A shuffle, a scuffle, but when I turned round
There was absolutely nothing there
Just bright green grass and clear fresh air.

I emptied my bag of paper and peels
And all the remains of all of my meals.
I put all my rubbish into the bin
And closed the lid. It made quite a din.

Then as I walked off, I heard a strange sound –
A shuffle, a scuffle, but when I turned round
This time it seemed there was something there!
I'm quite sure I spotted a massive brown bear!

By Jennifer Martin

Games around the world

Read about how to play different games from around the world.

People all over the world play different games. Have you ever heard of 'Gonggi nori' or 'Keeper of the Fire'?

Gonggi nori

Gonggi nori is a game from Korea. It is a game that you play with five small stones (or metal pieces, in a cross shape, called jacks).

This is how to play:

- Throw the stones or jacks onto the ground.
- Pick one up and throw it into the air.
- Quickly pick up another stone from the ground, and catch the one you threw up before it lands.

Then you can move on to the next round:

- Throw the two stones you have into the air.
- Try to pick up another stone and catch the two in the air before they land.

Now you have three stones, and you have to try to get four stones and then five in the same way.

When you have five stones, it is the final round:

- Throw the five stones into the air and try to catch them all on the back of your hand.
- The number you can catch is your final score.

When you don't get the correct number of stones, the next player gets a turn to try.

The winner is the person who has the highest score.

Keeper of the Fire

This is a traditional game from North America. Children try to remove sticks from the 'firekeeper', but they must not get caught. One person is the firekeeper. The firekeeper sits in the middle of a circle with a pile of sticks. The firekeeper wears a blindfold and keeps their hands in their lap.

The other players , who are called the 'raiders', quietly sneak up to the firekeeper and try to remove one stick from the pile. The firekeeper tries to touch the raiders while they do this. If the firekeeper touches a raider, that raider becomes the firekeeper.

The winner is the firekeeper when they touch a raider or the raider who can collect the most sticks.

Do you play any games that are similar to these?

Word games

What word games do you know?
Here's one you can play at school or at home.
Read the rules. Play the game with your group.

The same-letter word game

1. One person starts. The first player says a word or a person's name.

2. The next player has to find words to describe the word or name that is given. These words must begin with the same letter as the word or name.

3. Players get one point for every correct word they give.

4. If a player cannot think of a word, the next player in the group gets a turn.

5. The first player to get ten points is the winner.

Why do games need rules? What happens when someone doesn't follow the rules?

Ball.

Bouncing blue ball.

Carol.

Clever, caring Carol.

In the rainforest

Read this brochure to learn more about rainforests.

Rainforests are found near the equator in Africa, Asia, Australia and Central and South America. The largest rainforest in the world is the Amazon rainforest.

Join us on one of our spectacular rainforest tours!

My name is Carlos. I'm the guide for the night walking tours. If you want to go on an adventure of a lifetime, the rainforest is for you!

- You will learn about nature.
- You will get up close to plants and animals.
- You will make new friends and you will be left with wonderful memories!

What is the rainforest like?

Rainforests have four levels. Our tours take you through the understory layer. We are going to look up to the canopy and also examine the forest floor as we walk through this layer.

The emergent layer and tall canopy are like a roof of branches and leaves very high above the forest floor.

The floor is dark and damp because very little sunlight reaches it. Most of the floor is covered with rotting leaves and other decaying vegetation.

emergent layer

canopy

understory

floor

What animals live there?

Each level of the rainforest is home to different kinds of animals.

Monkeys, frogs, lizards, birds, snakes and sloths are found in the canopy and emergent layer.

Bigger animals such as forest elephants, tapirs, jaguars and leopards live in the understory layer.

Lots of insects and spiders live on the floor. This is also home to giant anteaters.

Would you like to take a walk through a rainforest at night? Why? / Why not?

What happens after dark?

At night the rainforest really comes alive.

All the bats wake up. They like to fly in the dark. They hunt moths and insects. A hungry bat eats hundreds of insects in a night.

Lightning bugs wink and shine like little lights. A lightning bug flashes its light on and off to say it is looking for a mate.

Lots of snakes come out at night. They can see in the dark. Some hunt on the ground. Some slide and slither up trees. If a snake sees a frog, it sneaks up and grabs it in its mouth.

Grasshoppers climb in the trees at night. They have long feelers to help feel their way in the dark and find plants to eat. Frogs, bats and tarantulas eat grasshoppers.

This tree frog has sticky fingers to help it climb trees. It can see in the dark and looks for moths, grasshoppers and small insects to eat.

Bugs Are Helpful

Read the poem to learn how bugs can be helpful.

Bugs!
We're everywhere.
We're in the water,
We're in the air.
Indoors, outdoors, underground,
Wherever you look that's where we're found.
We're on your hands and in your hair,
We're with you in the clothes you wear.
Bugs!
We can make your tummy funny,
Or a thousand noses runny.
Got a cut? Get a plaster.
Keep us out and you'll heal much faster.
We're the ones who make you ill,
Because of us you take that pill.
We're the ones who make you mad,
By turning good food into bad.
Bugs!
I agree, we don't sound good.
We cause more trouble than we should.
But ... let me tell you this about us,
People on Earth can't do without us.
In fact, you owe us such a lot!
If we weren't here to make things rot ...
... the piles of stuff you throw away
Would just get bigger every day.

What good things do bugs do? What bad things do they do?

Yes! We make things rot!
We make them smell!
Apple cores, potato skins,
All the scraps in all your bins –
We get to work and cause decay.
In time we rot it all away.
Rubbish mountains there would be,
If you didn't have my friends and me.
You need plants, and plants can't grow
Unless we're in the soil below.
We go to work on last year's leaves
Making food for next year's trees.
We get to work and cause decay,
In time we rot old leaves away.
Leaf mountains there would be,
If you didn't have my friends and me.
Bugs!
You can't see us,
But how you need us!
Because of all the work we do,
We make life possible for YOU.

By Sam McBratney

Animals from another time

Read about some of the strange animals that lived on Earth a very long time ago.

The Argentine bird or *Argentavis* (say: 'ar-jen-tay-vi')

The remains of this huge bird were found in Argentina, in South America. It lived there until about five million years ago.

The Argentine bird was the largest ever flying bird. It was 1.5 metres high. Its wings measured 7.5 metres across. Each wing feather could be as long as 1.5 metres.

This bird ate animals such as lizards, mice and rabbits. It also ate fish.

The Indrik Beast or *Indricotherium* (say: 'in-drik-oh-theer-ee-um')

This animal lived in Asia about 30 million years ago. It was the largest ever mammal to walk on land.

The very biggest of these creatures grew to about 4.5 metres high. It had a long neck that made it even taller, so that it could reach leaves high up in the trees.

It was also a very heavy animal. A really big one weighed 15,000 kilograms – that's much heavier than the largest rhino!

The mammoth (say: 'mam-oth')

The mammoth was a type of large elephant.

The bones of mammoths have been found in many different places. Those that lived in cold countries had long fur to keep them warm.

Mammoths grew up to three metres high. That is about the same size as today's elephants. They ate mostly grass and bushes. They had two long tusks which they used to protect themselves from attackers.

These animals are all extinct. What other extinct animals do you know about?

The Terror bird or *Titanis* (say: 'tee-tarn-is')

This giant bird lived about two million years ago in North America. It couldn't fly because it didn't have wings, but it did have arms covered in feathers.

This bird stood nearly three metres high and could run very fast. It was a meat eater and hunted small animals, using sharp claws and a very large beak to grip and kill them.

The giant short-faced kangaroo or *Procoptodon* (say: 'proh-kop-toe-don')

This animal lived in Australia. It weighed up to 200 kilograms – that's more than twice as heavy as today's biggest kangaroo.

Each of the creature's hind feet had one single large claw, like a hoof. Its long arms could stretch up over its head and its long, grabbing 'fingers' could reach leaves high up on trees. It was able to chew really tough leaves with its strong jaw.

The Great Fire of London

Look at the infographic about the Great Fire of London. Look at the pictures and graphs and read the information to find out about this historic event.

Fire can be very destructive, especially in crowded cities. One of the most famous fires of all time happened more than 350 years ago in the city of London.

FACTS and FIGURES

The fire began in a bakery on Pudding Lane just after midnight on Sunday 2nd September, 1666.
It burned for nearly four days.

87 out of 109 places of worship burned down.

80%

4/5 of the city was destroyed

+/- 500,000 people lived in London in 1666

There was not enough piped water.

People had to use buckets to try and put out the fire.

The city was very dirty and dry.

Many people were sick as a result of the plague.

THE BUILDINGS

The houses were made out of wood and straw.

Some houses were four storeys high.

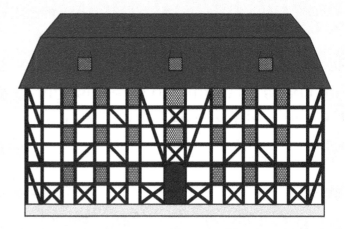

They were close together.

The streets were very narrow and crowded.

THE RESULT

+/- 100,000 people lost their homes

6 people died

It took nearly 50 years to rebuild the city.

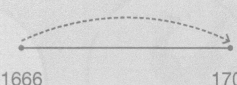

1666   1706

The new buildings were made of brick and stone.

Besides people and animals, what three things would you save first if there was a fire? Why?

Firefighters

Read about firefighters and the important work they do.

Fire keeps us warm and gives us light. But fire can be dangerous …
and that's why people are trained to be firefighters. Firefighters work as
a team and they have to train hard. Firefighters put out fires on land, at
sea and from the air.

Blowout!
An oil well fire can
burn like a huge,
flaming torch. This
is called a blowout.

Forest fires
Fires spread quickly
through forests.
Helicopters water-
bomb forest fires.

Will forests
always grow
again after a
fire?

Would you
like to be a
firefighter?
Why? / Why
not?

Chemical fires
Firefighters use foam to fight
chemical fires. The foam
stops smoke spreading.

Burning buildings
Firefighters use equipment like
fire engines and hosepipes to put
out these fires. They climb ladders
to reach the top of tall buildings.

Fire at sea
Firefighters use jet skis to put out fires on
small boats in shallow water. Big oil tanker
fires need fire boats with powerful hoses.

Fire safety!

Read these fire safety posters and discuss the information.

1. Don't play with matches and lighters. If you see matches or a lighter lying around, tell an adult.

2. If there's a fire in your house, GO OUTSIDE! Although fires are scary, NEVER hide in cupboards or under beds when there is a fire.

WAY OUT

3. If there's a fire, FALL and CRAWL. It is easier to breathe in a fire by staying low.

4. If your clothes are on fire, STOP, DROP and ROLL on the ground until the fire is out. Shout for help, but do not run. Running makes the flames burn faster.

5. Always have an escape route and practise using it. Check to see that doors and windows can open easily in case there is an emergency.

6. Choose a meeting place outside. NEVER go back into a burning building. If someone is missing, tell the firefighters. They have the right clothing and equipment to rescue people.

Fire Safety Rules

7. Know your emergency number.

What to do if there is a fire drill

- When you hear the alarm, stay calm and listen to instructions.
- Stop what you are doing and leave everything on your desk.
- Line up quickly. Don't run and don't push.
- Follow your teacher outside to the meeting point.
- Stay with your class at all times.
- When your teacher tells you it is safe, go back to class in an orderly fashion.

FIRE

Why are these rules important? What is your local emergency number for fires?

Puff, the Dragonsaurus

Dragons are known as brave creatures who breathe out fire. But they weren't always like that. Read this story to find out how they learned to do this.

Part One

Once upon a time, long, long ago, before the Moon was the Moon and the Sun was the Sun, a family of dragonsauruses (dragons for short) lived in a cave. The dragons were shy and they were scared of many things. They hid away from mice. They ran away from butterflies. They trembled when they heard the wind. In fact, most days they didn't leave their cave.

One cold, gloomy autumn day, the family of dragonsauruses woke up to the sound of an enormous crash. Worriedly, they peeped out of their cave. And what a sight met their eyes – outside their cave, stood a terrible beast. It stared at them and shouted loudly, 'Hey! Get lost. This is going to be my cave!'

Quick as a flash of lightning, the dragons fled to the back of their cave, trembling with fear. 'Oh what are we to do?' cried Mother. The family huddled together trying to work out what to do next.

'Er … Can I help?' asked Puff, a young dragon in the family.

'Hush, Puff,' replied his father, 'only grown-ups can solve this problem. You do want us to be safe, don't you? Just sit quietly. Go and read a book.'

Part Two

But Puff decided he was not going to read a book while his family was in danger! He turned around and crept out of the cave. Luckily, the beast was tired after all the shouting and was sleeping soundly. Puff crept carefully past it and ran as fast as the wind down the hill.

When Puff stopped to catch his breath, he looked up and saw an old tree.

'Excuse me,' said Puff, 'but do you know how to chase away scary beasts?' That made the tree laugh so much that many of her leaves fell off her branches.

'Oh dear me,' chuckled the tree, wiping tears from her eyes. 'You want to chase away a scary beast! That's so funny! Just look at you – a scaredy-cat dragon. That's so funny! Go away and read a book. You're making me lose all my leaves!'

And so Puff continued his journey sadly. He was feeling tired and thirsty by now, so he stopped next to a river and sat on a rock. 'Oi!' growled the rock crossly. 'Get off me!' Puff got such a fright he leaped into the air and nearly landed in the river!

'What are you doing here?' demanded the rock, rudely. 'Dragons never leave their cave.'

Puff told the rock all about the scary beast and the unhelpful tree. 'And you think you can help chase the beast away?' laughed the rock, loudly. 'Dear, dear me! That's so funny! Go away. You're making me laugh so much that I'm starting to crack! The tree was right – go and read a book.'

Part Three

Poor Puff sighed deeply. Would he ever be able to help his family? Would he ever be able to come up with a plan to chase away the monster? He decided to walk just a little further along the path before turning back to go home. A shiny berry on a bush caught his eye. It was red and sparkled like a ruby. Puff had never seen such a berry before (which was not surprising considering that he'd always stayed close to the cave). Curiously he picked it. Carefully he licked it. It didn't have a taste. Then he smelled it. It didn't have a scent. 'Is it safe to eat?' he wondered. Puff was so hungry he decided he'd take a bite. After all, what harm could one teeny tiny bite do?

Well, it did a lot! Puff thought his tongue was exploding. It felt like a fiery volcano had erupted in his mouth! He rushed back home, past the rude rock, past the chuckling tree, up the hill, back to his cave. 'Mum! Mum!' he screamed. 'I'm …' Puff stopped. To his complete amazement, fire was coming out of his mouth. He turned in shock and looked at the beast which by now was wide awake.

The beast's eyes grew wide with fear when it saw the flames coming from Puff's mouth. 'Help!' it screamed as it ran away. 'I'm being attacked by a fire-spitting dragon!'

And that's how Puff saved his family. It's also how dragons learned to breathe fire and become brave enough to leave their caves.

What type of story is this? How do you know it is not true?

By Jennifer Martin

Peter and the Wolf

Look at the pictures. What do you think happens in the story of Peter and the Wolf? Listen to this play script of the story, and follow along.

Peter and the Wolf is a traditional story about how a boy and his friends managed to outsmart a wolf that wanted to eat them.

NARRATOR: Peter lived with his grandfather in a small cottage near a forest. In front of the cottage lay a big, green meadow. Peter ran into the meadow and met his friend, Bird.

BIRD: Tweet! Hello, Peter. Have you come to play with me?

PETER: (bravely) No. I'm going into the forest to catch the big, bad wolf.

(A duck comes waddling into the meadow.)

DUCK: Quack! Quack! Don't go into the forest, Peter. Come and have a swim with me.

BIRD: TWEET! What kind of bird are you if you can't fly?

DUCK: Quack! Quack! What kind of bird are you if you can't swim?

BIRD: TWEET! TWEET!

DUCK: QUACK! QUACK!

PETER: Don't be silly. Duck's in the middle of the pond and you can't swim.

NARRATOR: Bird and Duck were arguing so much, they didn't see Cat come creeping up. Cat pounced at Bird …

CAT:	Grrr! MIAOW!
NARRATOR:	... but Bird flew up into the branches of a tall tree.
BIRD:	Nah, nah, nah-nah, nah! You can't catch me.
CAT:	Miaow! Well, I'll climb the tree and get Bird. (Cat stares at Bird at the top of the tree.)
NARRATOR:	Suddenly, Grandfather ran into the meadow, waving his arms. He looked very cross.
GRANDFATHER:	(angrily) Peter! I told you not to play in the meadow. It's a dangerous place! Go back home and stay there!
NARRATOR:	As soon as Peter and Grandfather had gone, a big, grey wolf came creeping out of the forest.
WOLF:	Ha ha ha! Peter's gone. Now I can catch my dinner! (The wolf creeps up on Cat.)
NARRATOR:	When Cat saw the wolf she jumped up into the tree.
CAT:	MIAOW! MIAOOOOW!
NARRATOR:	The wolf ran over to the pond. Duck saw the wolf, so she waddled out of the pond and tried to run away through the forest.
DUCK:	QUACK! QUACK!
WOLF:	Yummy! Duck dinner for me!
NARRATOR:	The wicked wolf snapped hold of Duck's tail ... and with one big gulp, he swallowed her up.
WOLF:	GULP! Slurp! Slobber!
NARRATOR:	High up in the tree, Cat and Bird looked down at the wolf. The wolf looked up at them.
WOLF:	(licking his lips) Yoo-hoo! I'm coming to get you too.

NARRATOR: But Peter had seen everything. He climbed out of his bedroom window and ran into the forest, carrying a strong rope.

PETER: (whispering to himself) I'm going to teach that wicked wolf a lesson.

(Peter scrambles up the tree where Bird and Cat are sitting.)

PETER: (in a low voice) Bird, go and fly around the wolf's head until he's sick and dizzy. And keep him near the bottom of the tree!

(Bird flies round and round the wolf's head.)

BIRD: WHEEEEEEE!

WOLF: Oi! Silly Bird. Go away. You're making me dizzy.

(Peter makes a lasso out of the rope, and dangles it down until it slips over the wolf's tail.)

NARRATOR: The wolf didn't see Peter … but he felt the lasso when it was pulled tight round his tail.

WOLF: OWW! What's that! Get off my tail!

(Peter ties the end of the rope round the thick branch he and Cat are sitting on – still high in the tree.)

PETER: Ha ha! I've got you, you big, bad wolf.

The Pied Piper of Hamelin

Look at the pictures. What do you think happens in the story? Then listen to the story. Did you predict what happens correctly?

The Pied Piper of Hamelin is a traditional story with a lesson. The story teaches that it is important to keep your promises.

Hamelin was full of rats.

The rats went into all the houses.

The Mayor and the people didn't know what to do.

The Piper arrived and the Mayor promised to pay him a lot of money.

The Piper played his flute
and the rats ran towards him.

The rats followed the
Piper out of the town.

The Mayor didn't want
to pay the Piper all the
money.

The Piper took the children
away from the town.

Help! The Sky Is Falling

Do you know the story of Chicken Licken? Read the poem with a partner. Take turns to read.

Chicken Licken was out one day,
Minding his business, I must say,
When a little acorn fell on his head
Chicken Licken thought he was soon to be
dead!

'The sky is falling – the end is near,
I must tell the queen – that is clear.
I must tell the queen, and the king too,
For they'll know exactly what to do.'

So off he hurried and soon met a friend
He told Henny Penny that the world would
soon end.
'Cluck cluck, Oh no – that cannot be,'
Said Henny Penny seriously.

'We must tell the queen, and the king too,
For they'll know exactly what to do.'
So off they hurried, and who did they meet?
Cocky Locky, alone in the street.

They told him the sky was falling down
'But we'll be crushed!' he said, with a frown.
'We must tell the queen, and the king too,
For they'll know exactly what to do.'

Foxy Loxy then walked by.
They told him about the falling sky.
'That's just awful. It's not OK,
Follow me – I know the way.'

They followed him high, they followed him low.
He seemed to know which way to go.
Round the corner, then back again,
And straight into the fox's den!

The Foxy family rubbed their tums
They picked their teeth and licked their gums

What do you think the lesson is in this story? Why?

And that was what happened to that silly bunch
They believed Chicky's story and ended up as lunch.

More about our world

You probably already know a bit about the Earth. Read this information to learn more about the continents.

Did you know that...

continents are huge pieces of land? There are seven continents today, but long ago they were all joined together. Scientists believe that the continents used to be one large piece of land about 250 million years ago. Scientists call this large continent Pangaea. They believe that Pangaea very slowly broke into pieces to form different continents. The continents slowly drifted apart from each other to where they are today.

Did you know that...

the continents are still moving? Believe it or not, North America and Europe are drifting apart by four centimetres per year. Scientists believe that in 50 million years from now, North and South America won't be joined together.

Did you know that...

there are five oceans in the world? The Pacific is the largest ocean. It is bigger than the Atlantic, the Indian, the Southern and the Arctic Oceans put together! The Pacific covers over one-third of the Earth's surface.

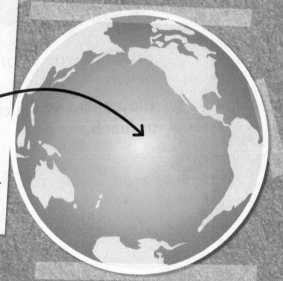

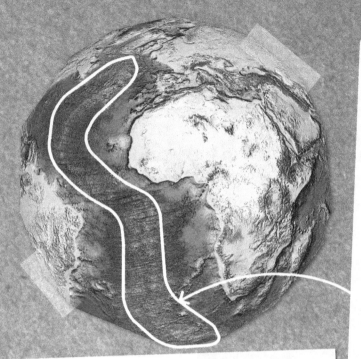

Did you know that...

there are mountains beneath the oceans? The longest mountain range in the world lies under the Atlantic Ocean. It stretches for almost 16 000 km and is called the Mid-Atlantic Ridge. Some of the mountains in this range are so tall they stick out of the water as islands.

Did you know that...

besides a valley in Antarctica, the Atacama desert is the driest place on Earth? It is so dry that in some parts of the desert it has not rained for hundreds of years. Can you imagine living in a place where it doesn't rain at all?

Did you know that...

the Amazon rainforest in South America is the biggest tropical rainforest in the world? The Amazon River flows through it. The river is the second longest in the world at 6 516 kilometres – only the Nile River is longer. More than 30 million plant and animal species live in rainforests.

Which mountains do you know about? Which is the highest mountain peak in the world? If you don't know, how could you find out?

Built wonders of the world

Which are the most famous structures in the world?

Read the information to learn more about some of the most famous and most visited structures in the world today.

Pyramids are massive ancient stone structures that are in different parts of the world. The most famous pyramids are the Great Pyramid at Giza in Egypt and the massive stepped pyramid in the Mayan ruins of Chichen Itza in Mexico.

No one knows for sure how people thousands of years ago built pyramids with only basic equipment. The stones are so big that engineers would find it difficult to move them today with modern equipment.

Petra is a famous city carved out of a sand stone cliff in Jordan. It is also called the Rose City because of the pink colour of the stone. Petra was the capital of the Nabataean empire of King Aretas IV who ruled from 9 BCE to 40 CE. The people of that time used technology wisely, and built huge tunnels and water chambers. They also built a theatre for 4 000 people!

The Colosseum in Rome is the largest stone amphitheatre ever built. It was built in 70 to 80 CE. It had seats at different levels so people could see clearly, and lots of entrances for them to reach their places easily. Most modern sports stadiums still use this design. Thousands of people watched many cruel fights and games there.

The Great Wall of China is the largest monument ever built. It is not actually one wall, though. Lots of different walls and forts join together to make it. These were built over a period of about 2 000 years. The wall is over 20 000 km long, and some people say that it can be seen from space (although astronauts on the International Space Station have said they could not see it). The Great Wall was originally a military barrier to protect China from invaders.

Machu Picchu is called 'the city in the clouds'. It was built in the 15th century, on the high slopes of the Andes Mountains in Peru. Historians believe that the Inca people built the city and that they left it later because many of them died from a terrible illness. The ruins were rediscovered in 1911, and today thousands of people climb the more than 3 000 steps to visit this amazing place.

The Taj Mahal at Agra in India is a more modern monument. This huge tomb is a famous example of Islamic art and architecture. The emperor built it in 1632 to remember his wife. The tomb is made of white marble and there are beautiful gardens with pools and fountains. More than three million people visit it each year.

Burj Khalifa in Dubai in the United Arab Emirates is one of the tallest structures in the world. The Burj, which opened in 2010, is 829.8 m tall and 160 storeys high. It is taller than all the other high buildings around it. Visitors can go up to levels 125 and 148 in glass elevators in just a few seconds. The view from these levels is amazing!

If you could choose three of these places to visit, which would you choose? Why?

Natural wonders of the world

People have built many wonderful things, but there are also many amazing natural places on Earth. Read about some of the natural places Li and her family have visited.

Li's scrapbook

Amazing places we've been to

Last year we went diving in the Komodo National Park in Indonesia. We also saw huge Komodo dragon lizards! I was surprised that they were so big!

This is the underground river at Palawan in the Philippines. The river flows through a huge cave. We went into the cave on a boat and learned about the cave and the animals in the national park.

Table Mountain is in South Africa. When the wind blows in a certain direction, the clouds cover the top of the mountain just like a table cloth! You can see more than 1 430 different plants at this site. We went to the top of the mountain in a cable car that turns around as it goes up.

Can you imagine cruising on a boat down the Amazon River! We did this for three days in a houseboat. The Amazon River flows through the largest rainforest in the world, and carries more water than the ten largest rivers in the world combined. That's a lot of water!

Ha Long Bay is in Vietnam. It is a huge bay. There are more than 1 900 small islands in the bay. Some of the islands are hollow caves. Many fishermen live in floating villages among the islands. Some of the islands are so big that they have their own lakes!

The Iguazu Falls are actually 275 separate waterfalls. The falls are 2 700 m wide. Parts of the Iguazu Falls are in Brazil, and the rest are in Argentina. We saw some amazing birds and a rainbow.

Jejudo is a volcanic island in South Korea. This dormant volcano is also the tallest mountain in South Korea. There are 360 smaller volcanoes around the main one. We took a hike to see the views over the bay.

Which natural places in your country are amazing? What makes them impressive?

The Olympics in ancient times

What do you know about the history of the Olympic Games?
Read the information below to find out more.

http://www.historyofolympics.com

The first ever Olympic Games took place in 776 BCE – more than 3 000 years ago! The ancient Olympic Games were very different to the modern ones we have today. The Olympic Games get their name from the ancient site of Olympia where the first games were held. Olympia was an important meeting place for the Greeks. We can still see the ruins of these ancient buildings today.

One day! One race!

The first Olympic Games took place on one day. The only event was a short running race from one end of the stadium to the other. The track was rough and wide and 20 people could run at the same time. Only men who spoke Greek were allowed to take part in the games.

Over the years, they added other events, and the games took place over four days. The events included wrestling, boxing, javelin and discus as well as horse and chariot races. At the 65th Olympics they introduced the hoplitodromos. This was a really tough running race! Men ran this race in full sets of armour and carried a heavy shield.

There was only one winner in each event, and there were no gold, silver and bronze medals like we have today. The winner received a wreath made of olive leaves as a prize and a statue was built in his honour.

Winners became very famous. One of the most famous Olympians was Leonidas of Rhodes. He won all three of the running races for four games in a row. He became a hero to all the Greeks.

The first woman to win an event was Kyniska of Sparta, who won the chariot racing event. However, she didn't officially take part in the Games! The rules said that the winner was the owner of the horse, not the rider.

The Olympics became very important in ancient Greece. At that time, the different cities in Greece were often at war. But the Olympics were so important that they stopped fighting before the Games so that the athletes could train in peace. The Greeks held Olympic Games regularly at Olympia until 393 CE, when the Roman emperor banned them.

Why do you think the Roman emperor banned the Olympic Games? Are the Olympic Games popular in your country? Why? / Why not?

From ancient to modern

Read the information below to learn more about the modern Olympic Games.

Baron Pierre de Coubertin was a Frenchman who thought it would be good to restart the Olympic Games. The first modern Olympics were in Athens, Greece, in 1896 and they now take place every four years in different host countries. Athletes from all over the world take part in the modern Olympic Games. Millions of people watch their achievements both at the events and on TV. Women competed in the Olympic Games for the first time in 1900.

The Olympic flag has five rings that intersect. Each ring is a different colour: red, black, green, blue and yellow. The rings represent the Americas, Australia, Africa, Asia, and Europe, and how they come together in the Olympic Games.

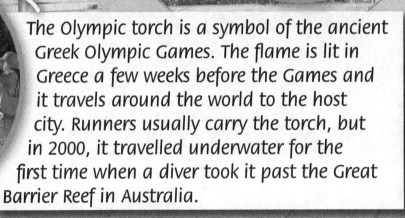

The Olympic torch is a symbol of the ancient Greek Olympic Games. The flame is lit in Greece a few weeks before the Games and it travels around the world to the host city. Runners usually carry the torch, but in 2000, it travelled underwater for the first time when a diver took it past the Great Barrier Reef in Australia.

At first, the Olympics took place only in the summer. The first Winter Olympics were in 1924, in Chamonix, France. In the Summer Games, athletes compete in around 30 different sports: on the track, on the road, on grass, in the water, on the water, in the open air and indoors. The running sprints are very popular. In the Winter Games, there are seven sports that take place on snow and ice, both indoors and outdoors.

Many athletes dream of taking part in the Olympic Games. They spend hours training and make many sacrifices to achieve their goals. The athletes that qualify for the Games are among the best in the world, and even if they do not win a medal, they are called Olympians.

Athletes who take part in the Olympic Games have to have special tests to make sure they have not used any medicines that might give them an advantage. These tests are called doping tests. For individual sports, such as athletics, all the athletes who are placed in the top five in any event have to have a doping test. Two further athletes in each event also have a test.

Why are doping tests important?

Going for gold!

Read about Usain Bolt - the world's fastest man.

Usain Bolt is one of the most famous athletes in the world. He comes from Jamaica and he was already winning track and field events there when he was just 14 years old. Usain Bolt was taller and faster than any of his competitors. In 2008, he set a new world record at the Olympic Games in Beijing. He ran 100m in 9.69 seconds, even though his shoe was untied! That year, Usain Bolt won two gold medals and also set new world records for all his races.

At the next Olympics, in 2012, he won three gold medals for three races, and he did this for a third time in 2016. This amazing achievement is called the 'triple double' – two gold medals at three Olympic Games in a row. Usain also won 11 events at the Track and Field World Championships, and during his career he broke many world records. Usain Bolt even has his own pose, called the 'Lightning Bolt'! Look at the picture above to see why.

Bolt: 'Worrying gets you nowhere. If you turn up worrying about how you're going to perform, you've already lost. Train hard, turn up, run your best and the rest will take care of itself.'

If you work hard, you will achieve success. Do you agree or disagree? Why?

Usain Bolt retired from competing in 2017. He now focuses on business, and running the Usain Bolt Foundation, a charity for children in Jamaica.

The odd Olympics

Some Olympic events are quite unusual! Read about some of the wackiest events from the past and present Olympics:

Rope climbing

In this event, competitors had to climb a rope using only their hands and arms. This event was included in the 1896, 1906, 1924 and 1932 Olympics. Can you imagine how challenging this is? Why do you think it was removed from the Olympic Games?

Skeleton sledding

This sport is included in the winter Olympics. Athletes travel headfirst down a freezing ice track at top speed on a small, hand-held sled, in a race to the finish line. The special sled is called a skeleton bobsled. A scary name for a scary sport!

Curling

In this sport, competitors slide granite stones across a sheet of ice to try and reach a target. Their teammates run ahead of the stones and use brooms to make the ice more slippery. Try to find more information about the sport of curling. Can you think of any sports that are similar?

Plunge for Distance

Plunge for distance only lasted one year as an Olympic sport (in 1904)! Athletes had to dive into a pool and float along for 60 seconds. At the end of one minute, officials measured the distance they floated to decide the winner.

Skijoring (say: skidge-err-ing)

Skijoring is skiing while being pulled along by an animal! Skiers are attached to their animals by a harness and towed along the snow. Skijoring was only included in the Olympic Games once, in 1928, and was won by competitors from Switzerland. But skijoring is still popular in many places.

In which of these events would you like to compete? Which ones would you avoid? Why?

Our eyes and ears

Read about the senses we use every day to make sense of our world.

Our senses are in action from the day we're born, and we use our senses to explore and learn about the world around us. We have five sense organs – eyes, ears, skin, nose and tongue. Sense organs are connected to the nervous system.

Everybody has the same five senses, but some people's senses are better than others. For example, some people can see really well, and others can hear very soft sounds.

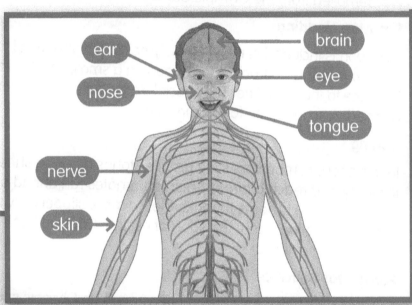

- ear
- nose
- brain
- eye
- tongue
- nerve
- skin

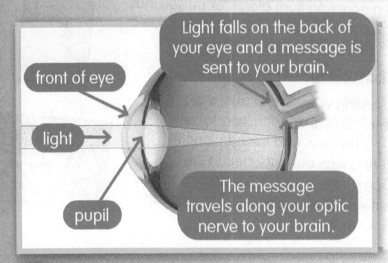

- front of eye
- light
- pupil

Light falls on the back of your eye and a message is sent to your brain.

The message travels along your optic nerve to your brain.

Humans can see in colour. Many animals see only in shades of black and white.

But, humans can only see colour when there's lots of light. If we go outside at night, we can only see in black and white.

Sounds are made when something vibrates (moves). For example, a guitar makes a sound when you pluck the strings.

Your ears hear the sounds and send them into a tube called an ear canal. They reach your eardrum and make it vibrate. The vibrations pass to your cochlea (say: 'kok-lee-uh'). This is a tube that looks like a snail's shell. Inside your cochlea, liquid moves tiny hairs that send messages along nerves to your brain.

Your ears help you to balance. When you move your head, liquid inside the semicircular canals moves too. At the same time, your eyes are sending information to your brain. Your brain uses all this information to move your arms and legs and stop you falling over.

When you spin around, lots of messages from your eyes and ears are sent to your brain. Your brain gets confused and you feel dizzy.

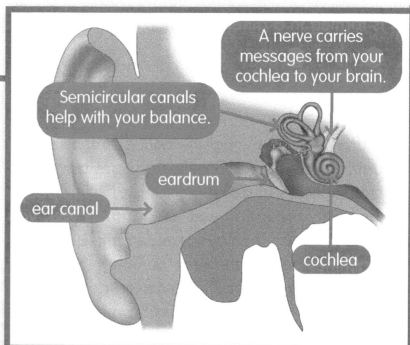

A nerve carries messages from your cochlea to your brain.

Semicircular canals help with your balance.

eardrum

ear canal

cochlea

Which sense do you think is the most important? Why?

Braille – reading by feeling

Robert loves reading. However, Robert is blind, so he reads a special alphabet called braille with his fingertips. Read what he says about reading in braille.

You read braille with your fingertips. The letters are actually little bumps on the page, and each letter is formed in a different pattern.

Today, a special machine called a braille embosser prints many books. Braille signs are also found in public places to make it easier for blind people to find their way around. If you look around you, you might find braille on the keys of automatic banking machines and on the floor numbers in a lift. You may even find a raised dot on the J key and the number 5 on a computer keyboard.

I read my school books in braille, but I also listen to audiobooks, and my mum often reads aloud to me. I really enjoy that.

At my school we use special computer programs to help us.

The keyboard has braille letters and the programme speaks the words on the screen. So, if I type in an email, the computer reads it out as I type so that I can check my work. When I go to a website, the computer reads out the text on the screen.

Some people are legally blind. This means they are not completely blind but they can only see very little. They sometimes read special books with very large print. Electronic readers also help them as they can make the print as big as they need it.

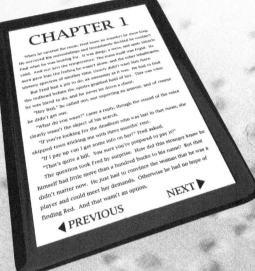

An electronic reader

Think about what it is like to be blind or to have low vision. How do blind people do everyday things?

Helen Keller

Read about Helen Keller and her achievements.

1880

1880 Helen is born in Alabama in the USA. She starts talking at the age of six months.

1882 Helen gets a fever and becomes blind and deaf.

1885 Her parents do research to try and help their daughter.

1887 Anne Sullivan, a teacher, comes to live with the family to teach Helen to communicate with others.

1890 Helen goes to speech classes at a school for deaf children.

1902 Helen writes her first book, *The Story of My Life.*

1904 Helen is the first deaf and blind person to graduate with distinction from college.

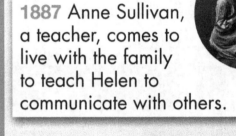

1920 Helen works hard to tell other people about deafness and blindness, and to help others. She travels and writes more books and is awarded several degrees.

1920

Helen Keller was born on June 27th, 1880, in Tuscumbia, Alabama. She grew up on her family's large farm which was called Ivy Green.

She was not born blind and deaf; at nineteen months old she became very sick and lost her hearing and her sight. For a child this was very frustrating, and Helen became very angry when she could not communicate with her family. She kicked and screamed. But Helen did not give up. She communicated with her family in her own way, using signs. When she wanted to say that she was cold, she would shiver.

When Helen was six years old, Anne Sullivan came to stay with Helen's family as her teacher. Anne wanted to teach Helen to communicate, but it was not easy to do. One day, Anne let water run over Helen's hand. Then she traced w-a-t-e-r on Helen's hand. Helen understood – the letters spelled 'water'. Helen learned many other words that day!

'The best and most beautiful things in the world cannot be seen nor even touched, but just felt in the heart.'   *Helen Keller, 1891*

Helen learned to read books in braille. She also learned to write and speak. She used a special typewriter to write her first book.

Helen wanted to go to college. She attended Radcliffe College (Harvard University), and Anne Sullivan went with her to help her to do well at the college.

Helen Keller lived to be 88 years old and she spent her life helping people to understand about deafness and blindness. She also helped many other deaf and blind people learn to communicate.

How do you think Helen Keller felt as she was growing up?

Fashion forward!

Jonathan loves clothes. He spends all day thinking about fabrics, textures, and patterns and imagining new clothes. One Tuesday morning in the school holidays, Jonathan decides it's time to go shopping. Read on to find out what happens:

Jonathan and his mum are going shopping today.
Jonathan is very excited. His mum is not.
Mum appears at the top of the stairs.
She looks tired.
'Are you ready to go?' asks Jonathan.
'Do we have to?' grumbles Mum.

Twenty minutes later, Jonathan and his mum are in his favourite shop.
'Jonathan, what do you think of this blue jumper?'
'I like the pattern, but I don't like the colour.'
'Oh.'

Mum looks around the shelves.
'What about this orange jacket?'
'I don't like how it fits!'
'And these yellow trousers?'
'They don't have my size!'

Jonathan is very difficult to shop with. Mum is very tired.

'Jonathan, do you like any of the clothes in this entire shop?'

Jonathan looks around.
'I don't think so!'

Jonathan doesn't like any clothes at the next shop, or the shop after that, or the shop after that. Mum gets cross. She has to go to work in the afternoon, and they still haven't found any clothes.

Later, Gran finds Jonathan in his room. He is upset.

'I know what I want to wear, but I just can't find it!'

Gran has an idea.

The next morning they go shopping together, just Gran and Jonathan. Mum is relieved. When Mum comes home, she hears a funny whirring sound in the kitchen. Mum peeks around the corner.

She sees Gran and Jonathan at the sewing machine. There is a huge pile of fantastic, differently coloured fabrics next to them. Jonathan is smiling while he sews. He sees Mum, and holds up his sewing project: a yellow patterned T-shirt. 'Hey, Mum! I know what I want to be when I grow up! A fashion designer!'

What colours and patterns do you like?

Mum is happy that she doesn't have to go shopping for Jonathan any more. She reaches up to close the kitchen curtain and finds...

... a giant T-shirt-shaped hole in it! 'Jonathan!' Gran giggles. Jonathan shrugs. 'The pattern was perfect!'

Jia's diary

Dear Diary,

Today was the WORST DAY EVER! My brother Jihu and I started at OUR new school, and it was awful. First, at assembly, the head teacher called out our names and asked us to stand up in front of everyone. When I stood up, I tripped over Jihu's foot, and fell over. I was very embarrassed.

Jihu is never embarrassed. He is very confident. At break time, he talked to some of the boys in his class, and then he played football with them. I was too shy to talk to anyone! This morning, my mum said I should not be nervous to start at a new school, because I have my twin brother with me. She doesn't understand. I'm happy that he is making new friends, but I feel very lonely. Making friends is difficult, especially because I am bad at sports. In English class, I was too scared to answer any questions, so I drew a new manhwa comic. My teacher got very angry because I was not listening to her. I miss my old teachers, and my friends! I am worried that I will not make new friends because I am not as cool as my brother Jihu.

My parents say this new school is better, but I wish I could go back to my old school. I was in a club for music, with my best friend, Eun, and we used to sing traditional Arirang songs together. Here I am all alone, except for Jihu, and my comics.

I hope things get better!
Love,
Jia

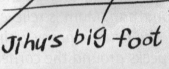

Jihu's big foot

angry teacher!

My Comics

What things can you do to help new students in your school?

Clubs

Look at all the adverts on the noticeboard at Jia's new school.

City Dance Academy

Join City Dance Academy NOW!

Hip-hop on Tuesdays and Thursdays @ 16h00
Modern dance on Tuesdays and Thursdays @ 18h00
Salsa on Mondays, Wednesdays @ 16h00
FREE DANCE PARTY EVERY FRIDAY @ 19h00

Contact info@citydance for more details. $5 per class, or $45 for 11 classes!

Football Club!

JOIN US ON TUESDAYS AT 5PM

SPEAK TO MISS PARK TO SIGN UP.

Join the COMIC CLUB!

Learn all about comics, from manga, to manhwa, to Marvel, and more!

Every Monday and Wednesday at 5pm in Mr Lee's classroom

Film Club

This week's film: MAKING MUSIC 3 starring Shawn Mendies and Adriana Grand!

Come and watch the film and our discussion afterwards!
Next Monday, 14th october, at 16:00.

School Social!

HAVE FUN AND MAKE NEW FRIENDS!

It's the School Social event this Friday (7pm).

Which of these activities interest you? Which clubs would you join?

A Future Celebrity Chef?

Staff reporter: Mick Orkins
Wed Oct 14, 2020
MELBOURNE, AUSTRALIA

The final round of the Young Chef competition 2020 took place last night in Melbourne. And the winner is someone who may become one of the celebrity chefs of the future. In the ten-week long competition, she never panicked, she baked the most original and tasty meals – and she made lots of friends. Her name is Sophia Wang.

Before the final I interviewed Sophia at her home. I wanted to know how she became interested in cooking.

'It all started with washing the dishes - the only time my mum let me be alone in the kitchen! I was washing the dishes when I saw an advertisement for the Young Chef competition on TV. It looked like so much fun.'

Then I asked about when she had decided to enter the competition.

'I started thinking about things that I could cook. Then my mum came in and said, "What were you thinking when you washed this pot? It's not clean." So I told her. She was not sure at first. But I managed to convince her!'

Sophia has some experience in the kitchen. Her dad is Chinese and they often make traditional dumplings together as a family. The traditional dumplings she made on the show were a favourite with all the judges. She also often makes cakes with her brother.

Throughout the competition and the interview, Sophia laughed and smiled.
Sophia Wang - Remember that name!

Can you tell what the writer thinks about Sophia?

Headlines!

A good news report won't give the writer's own opinion or support one side of a story more than the other side.

Read the newspaper headlines below. Which headlines tell us about what the writer thinks?

Hero fights for justice after wrongful arrest

5-year-old boy injured by dangerous fence at park

Rude customer banned from local supermarket by brave employee!

Leather jackets are bad fashion – here's why

200% increase in traffic this year – statistics confirm

What's the writer's opinion in each headline?

Anjali's diary

Read Anjali's diary about her holiday.

Anjali and her family went on a safari in Africa. It was the first time that they had seen animals in the wild and they enjoyed their holiday in the game reserve.

Look at the zebra patterns carefully. What differences can you find?

Home   Insert   Design

B *I* U abe X₂ X² A A A

Monday

Today we met our tour guide, Jabu. He knows a lot about animals. He took us on a game drive to a water hole. We had to sit very quietly in the Land Rover so that we did not scare the animals away.

Jabu told us that every zebra has its own striped pattern and that they sleep standing up. Now I understand why zebra crossings in towns and cities have their name!

Tuesday

Today was very cloudy and windy, so I took a blanket with me in the van. We left for our game drive very early this morning. Everyone was yawning and sleepy, but not for long! Jabu took us deep into the bush and we were lucky enough to see a lot of animals. Jabu stopped the Land Rover and told us to keep very still. He stared at a tree. I thought he was being silly, but when I looked carefully, I saw a beautiful leopard lying fast asleep on a branch. Not many people get to see a leopard in the wild!

Wednesday

We spent most of the day at the campsite because it was too hot to go out on a drive. Jack and I made friends with some of the other children. We had lots of fun swimming in the pool. One of the little girls was being very naughty and kept on splashing us! There were lots of monkeys in the trees. Some of them had babies. I liked watching them.

Thursday

Jabu took us out for a hike today. We saw many different plants and trees. We also saw a bright green snake! We had to drink lots of water and wear hats and sunblock.

Friday

Today was our last day. I was feeling sad because I had not yet seen a lion. It was my dream to see the king of the wild. We went for our last drive, and there, on the side of the road, we saw a lioness and her cubs. They were so sweet! I took a lot of photos!

Which wild animals would you most like to see? Where could you see them in the wild?

Island fun

Adverts try to convince you to buy something by making it sound attractive. Read this advertisement for a summer holiday.

Call us today on 123-234-5678 or visit our website
www.islandhoppers.sun
Special offers for early bookings. Don't wait. Don't leave it too late!

Sun, Sand and Sea – it doesn't get better than this!

Relax in the sun.
Dig in the sand.
Play in the clear blue sea and swim
with dolphins.

Leave the shopping centres behind.
Make new friends. Learn to surf. Catch fish.
Collect shells.
Have the best time ever!

Island Hoppers can make this happen.

How does this advert try to make the holiday sound good?

An island holiday

What do you need for a summer holiday on an island? Look at the things below.

Pair of swimming goggles and a snorkel

A sun umbrella

A towel

A sun hat

Pair of warm socks

Bottle of mosquito repellent

Bottle of sunblock

A woollen beanie hat

A water bottle

Pair of snow boots

Pair of flip-flops

A swimming costume

Pair of woolly gloves

A snowsuit

Which things would you pack for a beach holiday in a hot place? Which items would you leave behind? Why?

Holiday island activities

Look at this map. Read all the different activities you can do on this holiday island.

What other activities can you do on an island holiday?

	Sunbathing
	Swimming
	Snorkelling
	Shopping
	Hiking/Walking
	Surfing
	Swimming with dolphins
	Horseriding
	Sailing
	Cycling
	Birdwatching

Which activities would you like to do on this island? Which would you avoid doing?

Where will you go?

Read the text messages these children sent their friends. Can you work out which country each person is visiting?

I'm sending you this message from the very top of the Eiffel Tower. It is amazing up here and you can see the whole city. We're going to the Louvre Museum tomorrow.

It is really amazing here. The sun shines for about 22 hours every day. It hardly gets dark at all. There are reindeer here and we went on a boat on a fjord yesterday.

I'm near the top of the boot-shaped country. We went to visit the Leaning Tower of Pisa, it really does lean over. I took a photo that looks like I am holding it up.

If you could go anywhere in Europe, where would you go? Why?

You'll never believe where I've just been. It is the largest stone amphitheatre ever built and modern stadiums are still built in this style. Can you guess?

Read these two poems about different cities in Europe.

Paris

Glittering, busy

Rushing, twinkling, driving,

Taking photos of the Eiffel Tower

Posing, laughing, clicking

Walking, shopping, waiting

Beautiful, fashionable

City

> Look at the poems again. Talk about how they are structured.

Barcelona

Bright, exciting

Walking, staring, smiling

Admiring amazing buildings

Feeling lost quite often

Directions, maps

Home

William Collins' dream of knowledge for all began with the publication of his first book in 1819.

A self-educated mill worker, he not only enriched millions of lives, but also founded a flourishing publishing house. Today, staying true to this spirit, Collins books are packed with inspiration, innovation and practical expertise.

They place you at the centre of a world of possibility and give you exactly what you need to explore it.

Collins. Freedom to teach.

Published by Collins
An imprint of HarperCollinsPublishers
The News Building
1 London Bridge Street
London
SE1 9GF

HarperCollins Publishers
Macken House,
39/40 Mayor Street Upper,
Dublin 1, DO1 C9W8,
Ireland

Browse the complete Collins catalogue at
www.collins.co.uk

© HarperCollinsPublishers Limited 2021

10 9 8 7 6 5

ISBN 978-0-00-836913-2

British Library Cataloguing-in-Publication Data

A catalogue record for this publication is available from the British Library.

Author: Jennifer Martin and Karen Morrison
Publisher: Elaine Higgleton
Series Editor: Daphne Paizee
Product Manager: Lucy Cooper
Development Editor: Cait Hawkins
Project Manager: Lucy Hobbs
Proof reader: Michael Lamb
Cover design: Gordon MacGilp
Cover artwork: QBS Learning
Internal design: Ken Vail Graphic Design
Typesetter: QBS Learning
Illustrations: QBS Learning and Beehive Illustrations
Production controller: Lyndsey Rogers
Printed and bound in the UK by Ashford Colour Ltd.

With thanks to the following teachers and schools for reviewing materials in development: Hawar International School; Melissa Brobst, International School of Budapest; Niki Tzorzis, Pascal Primary School Lemessos.

Acknowledgements

The publishers gratefully acknowledge the permissions granted to reproduce copyright material in the book. Every effort has been made to contact the holders of copyright material, but if any have been inadvertently overlooked, the Publisher will be pleased to make the necessary arrangements at the first opportunity.

HarperCollinsPublishers Limited for extracts and artwork from:

Bugs! by Sam McBratney, illustrated by Eric Smith, text © 2010 Sam McBratney. Animal Ancestors by Jon Hughes, text © 2006 Jon Hughes. Peter and the Wolf by Diane Redmond, illustrated by John Bendall-Brunello, text © 2007 Diane Redmond. The Pied Piper of Hamelin by Jane Ray, illustrated by Jane Ray, text © 2011 Jane Ray. Chicken Licken by Jeremy Strong, illustrated by Tony Blundell, text © 2007 Jeremy Strong. The Ultimate World Quiz by Claire Llewellyn , text © 2008 Claire Llewellyn. The Olympic Games by John Foster, text © 2009 John Foster. Your Senses by Sally Morgan, illustrated by Maurizio De Angelis, text © 2012 Sally Morgan.

Photo acknowledgements

The publishers wish to thank the following for permission to reproduce photographs. Every effort has been made to trace copyright holders and to obtain their permission for the use of copyright materials. The publishers will gladly receive any information enabling them to rectify any error or omission at the first opportunity.

(t = top, c = centre, b = bottom, r = right, l = left)

p4t bikeriderlondon/Shutterstock, p4b photobyphotoboy/Shutterstock, p5t varuna/Shutterstock, p5b Tyler Olson/Shutterstock, p9 (background t) Lereen/Shutterstock, p9 (background b) atsiana Selivanava/Shutterstock, p9 (letter tiles) Pinone Pantone/Shutterstock, p11b Jim Cumming/Shutterstock, p16 (pie chart) Tikhonov/Shutterstock, p16-17 (background) Marcin Wos/Shutterstock, p18tr Tom Reichner/Shutterstock, p18tl urraheeshutter/Shutterstock, p18br curraheeshutter/Shutterstock, p18bl Lumppini/Shutterstock, p18b Serg_Kr/Shutterstock, p19 Ienabsl/Shutterstock, p19br VOLYK IEVGENII/Shutterstock, p30t Niki Whitehorn, p30b Niki Whitehorn/, p31t NGDC, p31c John Warburton-Lee/Alamy, p31b Jon Arnold Images Ltd/Alamy, p32t Mohamed Hakem/Shutterstock, p32b Maciek A/Shutterstock, p33t Lestertair/Shutterstock, p33c SF photo/Shutterstock, p33b SL-Photography/Shutterstock, p34t Fancy Friday/Shutterstock, p34c Alexandra Lande/Shutterstock, p34b Thasneem/Shutterstock, p35t Ethan Daniels/Shutterstock, p35c Nico Wijaya/Shutterstock, p35c (boat) Edmund Lowe Photography/Shutterstock, p35c (diver) SARAWUT KUNDEJ/Shutterstock, p35b Crystal Egan/Shutterstock, p36t Daleen Loest/Shutterstock, p36c lessandro Zappalorto/Shutterstock, p36b PhotoRoman/Shutterstock, p37t Junior Braz/Shutterstock, p37b Narumon Srisirisavad/Shutterstock, p40-41 (background) Petr Toman/Shutterstock, p40t Shahjehan/Shutterstock, p40c Shahjehan/Shutterstock, p40b Ruslans Golenkovs/Shutterstock, p41t Iurii Osadchi/Shutterstock, p41c Leonard Zhukovsky/Shutterstock, p42t (also inset on p3) Ververidis Vasilis/Shutterstock, p42b Celso Pupo/Shutterstock, p43t The History Collection/Alamy, p43ct Leonard Zhukovsky/Shutterstock, p43c Dan POTOR/Shutterstock, p43cb The History and Art Collection/Alamy, p43b energy1/Shutterstock, p46-47 (background) Coprid/Shutterstock, p46-47 wavebreakmedia/Corbis Historical/Shutterstock, p47tr iQoncept/Shutterstock, p48tr Historical/Hulton Archive/Getty, p48br Hulton Deutsch/Archive Photos/Getty, p48bl Topical Press Agency/Stringer/Getty, p49 Fred Stein Archive/Contributor/Getty, p53 (background) Valentin Agapov/Archive Photos/Ss/Shutterstock, p54l Thiranun Kunatum/Shutterstock, p54r Illin Denis/Shutterstock, p55tr GraphicaArtis /Corbis Historical/Getty, p56-57, 58 (background) tratong/Shutterstock, p56 (also inset on p3) GTS Productions/Shutterstock, p57t BlueOrange Studio/Shutterstock, p57b Marci Paravia/Shutterstock, p58tl Doctoresa/Shutterstock, p58tc iSiripong/Shutterstock, p58tr rtmiles/Shutterstock, p58b Rene Blanc/Shutterstock, p59l Brian A. Witkin/Shutterstock, p59c Tory Kallman/Shutterstock, p59r NadyaEugene/Shutterstock, p59 (background) BlueOrange Studio/Shutterstock, p62t Thanapong Suthin/Shutterstock, p62ct Svetography/Shutterstock, p62cb Mike Mareen/Shutterstock, p62b Farbregas Hareluya /Shutterstock, p63t Ivan Mateev/Shutterstock, p63tc Sergey Kelin/Shutterstock, p63c auro Rodrigues/Shutterstock, p63bl spatuletail/Shutterstock, p63br s74/Shutterstock